KINDLE MONEY MAKING VICTORY

Discover How To Make Money From Your Kindle EBooks Successfully

Dominic. B. Frost

Dominicbfrost.com

Copyright © 2018 Dominic. B. Frost
All rights reserved.
ISBN-13: 978-1986273640
ISBN-10: 1986273644

COPYRIGHT

February 2018 Edition
Copyright © 2018 by Dominic. B. Frost All rights reserved.

No part of this book may be reproduced in any form or by any electronic or mechanical means including information storage and retrieval systems except in the case of brief quotations in articles or reviews - without the permission in writing from its publisher, Dominic. B. Frost.

DISCLAIMER

All brand names and products names used in this book are trademarks, or trade names or their respective holders. I am not associated with any product or vendor in this book.

The information provided herein is stated to be truthful and consistent, in that any liability, in terms of inattention or otherwise, by any usage or abuse of any policies, processes, or direction contained within is the solitary and utter responsibility of the recipient reader.

Under no circumstances will and legal responsibility or blame be held against the publisher and author for any reparation, damages, or monetary loss due to the information herein, either directly or indirectly.

Please note the information contained within this document is for educational and entertainment purposes only. Every attempt has been made to provide accurate, up to date and reliable, complete information. No warranties of any kind are expressed or implied. Readers acknowledge that the author is no engaging in the rendering of legal financial, medical or professional advice.

By reading this document, the reader agrees that under no circumstance are we responsible for any losses, direct or indirect which are incurred as a result of the use of information contained within this document, including but not limited to, -errors, omissions or inaccuracies.

TABLE OF CONTENT

INTRODUCTION — 1

ESSENTIAL INFORMATION
YOU NEED TO KNOW ABOUT
MAKING MONEY FROM YOUR KINDLE EBOOKS — 2

CREATE AND SELL A
PAPERBACK VERSION OF YOUR KINDLE EBOOKS — 5

CREATE AND SELL AN
AUDIOBOOK VERSION OF YOUR KINDLE EBOOKS — 9

ENROL IN THE
AMAZON KDP SELECT EXCUSIVITY AGREEMENT — 14

RUN A KINDLE COUNTDOWN DEAL — 16

SELL THE FILM AND
TELEVISION RIGHTS TO YOUR KINDLE EBOOKS — 20

USING YOUR WEBSITE
TO MAKE MONEY FROM YOUR KINDLE EBOOKS — 40

PROMOTE YOUR KINDLE EBOOKS ON YOUR WEBSITE — 42

CREATE AND SELL YOUR
OWN MERCHANDIZE ON YOUR WEBSITE — 43

PROVIDE AND SELL A SERVICE ON YOUR WEBSITE — 46

CREATE AND SELL A
MEMBERSHIP SERVICE ON YOUR WEBSITE — 49

USE A DROP SHIPPING
SERVICE TO SELL PRODUCTS ON YOUR WEBSITE — 56

BUY AND SELL
WHOLESALE PRODUCTS ON YOUR WEBSITE   59

PROMOTE AFFILIATE
PRODUCTS AND SERVICES ON YOUR WEBSITE   61

INSERT ADVERTS WITHIN YOUR WEBSITE   81

WHICH METHODS SHOULD YOU USE TO MAKE
MONEY FROM YOUR KINDLE EBOOKS AND WEBSITE   85

CONCLUSION   87

INTRODUCTION

Firstly I'd like to say thank you for buying my book.

I hope that with this book you will be able to take the steps needed to make money from the Kindle eBooks you've created and not just by selling them online but also by other means.

You will firstly learn and how it takes time and work in order to make money from your Kindle eBooks.

You'll then learn about converting your Kindle eBooks into other format, how you can use your enrolment in KDP Select to make money from your Kindle eBooks, how you can sell the film and television rights to your Kindle eBooks to make money and finally you will learn how you can use your Kindle eBooks to drive traffic to your website and use that traffic in order to make some money.

You should also read my [Kindle Writing and Publishing Victory](#) book if you haven't created any Kindle eBooks which will give you advice on the type of Kindle eBooks you should write, which topic or genre to choose from, the research you need to carry out, what you shouldn't do when writing your Kindle eBooks, how to upload your Kindle eBooks and much much more.

Finally I'd like to say thank you once again for buying my book.

Dominic. B. Frost

[Dominicbfrost.com](#)

Facebook: [https://www.facebook.com/Dominic-B-Frost-1486663614766022/](#)

Twitter: [https://twitter.com/DominicBFrost](#)

ESSENTIAL INFORMATION YOU NEED TO KNOW ABOUT MAKING MONEY FROM YOUR KINDLE EBOOKS

The methods within my Kindle Money Making Victory Book will show you how you can make money by publishing your very own Kindle eBooks.

However it will take time and work in order for you to earn any money from your Kindle eBooks as most of the companies will be holding onto the money you make from their programs for sixty to ninety days to ensure that refunds are paid back if the customer doesn't like your Kindle eBooks and products/services you're selling/promoting.

So the whole idea of you making a lot of money fast by using some of the methods with my Kindle Money Making Victory book is a dream.

But if you work hard at creating Kindle eBooks, you keep creating good Kindle eBooks regularly, you use some of the methods within my Kindle Money Making Victory book to make some money from your Kindle eBooks and you market your Kindle eBooks successfully then you can expect to make some money.

How Much Money Will I Make?

I can't answer how much you'll make as it's all down to how good your Kindle eBooks are, how you market your Kindle eBooks, what methods you use to make money from your Kindle eBooks, how many Kindle eBooks you've created and how many Kindle eBooks you regularly publish.

How Soon Can I Expect To Make Money from My

Kindle eBooks?

Again Amazon and the other methods within my Kindle Money Making Victory book will mostly hold onto any sales and earnings you make for at least 60 days.

This is due to refunds and any other issues that may occur.

Also when you first start creating, publishing and marketing your Kindle eBooks the money you make will flow slowly.

So at first you'll either make no money or a very small amount of money but as time goes by and with more Kindle eBooks you published and marketed regularly you'll start to see some money trickle in each month until you start to make a passive income.

What Is a Passive Income?

A passive income is basically where you receive money from your previous work on a regular basis which will require very little work in order to maintain.

So After a While I Won't Have to Work In Order To Make Money from My Kindle eBooks?

No you will still have to work at creating, publishing and marketing Kindle eBooks in order to receive and maintain a passive income.

You may be able to slow down the creating, publishing and marketing of your Kindle eBooks but you should never stop.

If you do stop then your passive income will slowly decrease over time until you'll either receive very little or no income at all.

You may also see dips in your passive income.

For instance if you have previously published some Kindle eBooks before and have some loyal readers and buyers and then you publish a new Kindle eBook then your new Kindle eBook sales will increase which will also increase the passive income you make.

However after a few days go by then that high dip in your sales and readers will dip back down until it levels off.

So This Isn't A Passive Income?

In a way it is because you will receive regular income from your previous work which will increase and decrease but you will still need to work at creating publishing and marketing your past and future Kindle eBooks in order to receive this income.

There also maybe some Kindle eBooks which will sell whether you market them or not due to their popularity however I still recommend you create and market your Kindle eBooks regularly.

CREATE AND SELL A PAPERBACK VERSION OF YOUR KINDLE EBOOKS

Creating a Paperback version of your Kindle eBooks is one of the straightforward methods you can use to make some extra money from Amazon.

How Do I Create a Paperback Version of My Kindle eBooks?

You'll firstly need to format your Paperback books manuscript differently to the way you formatted your Kindle eBooks manuscript because your readers won't be able to click on the table of content links to go to a specific chapter.

So you should give each page a number and add the first page to each chapter within the table of content.

You'll then need to change your margins and create blank pages so that your chapters begin on the right side rather than the left.

Finally you'll need to change the format of your manuscript file to PDF which can easily be done in Microsoft Word by going to save as and changing the file type to pdf.

More information on formatting can be found at https://www.createspace.com/Products/Book/InteriorPDF.jsp and https://www.createspace.com/Products/Book/#content3.

What Should I do After I've Created a Paperback Version of My Kindle eBooks?

You need create a Paperback book cover which should look similar to your Kindle eBook cover but with a back cover and synopsis.

You can easily create a Paperback book cover by either by using the following tools.

- Amazon cover creator
- Createspace cover creator
- Canva
- other tools available at http://dominicbfrost.com/paperback-cover-design-software-and-resources/

Or you can hire a Paperback book cover designer to create one for you.

I have a list of websites you can use to hire a Paperback book cover designer at http://dominicbfrost.com/freelance-job-posting-and-hiring-websites/.

How Do I Upload My Paperback Books And Make Them Available To Buy?

To upload and sell your Paperback books you'll need to do the following.

1. Create/log into your Createspace account at https://www.createspace.com/ and select the add new title link or use an alternative Paperback book publishing service listed at http://dominicbfrost.com/paperback-print-on-demand-book-services/.
2. Enter all the details of your Paperback book details.
3. Upload your Paperback book manuscript.
4. Create or upload your Paperback book cover.
5. Price your Paperback book.
6. Select where you want to distribute your Paperback book.
7. Publish your Paperback book.

How Much Should I Price My Paperback Books?

Createspace and other Paperback book publishing services will set a minimum amount you will need to charge for the sale of your Paperback books so that they can cover the printing, packaging and posting costs.

This will mean your Paperback books will be priced higher than your Kindle eBooks which most people on Amazon and other marketplaces expect.

However you shouldn't price your Paperback books to the minimum amount as you'll barely make any profit.

You also shouldn't price your Paperback books too high otherwise people won't buy them at all.

So I recommend you price your Paperback books based on how much profit you would make for the sale of your Kindle eBooks.

So if you make $2.00 for each of your Kindle eBooks being sold and the minimum price of your Paperback books is $5.00 then you should price your Paperback books to around $7.00 so you would make $2.00 profit for each Paperback book sold.

However how you price your Paperback books is completely up to you.

Where should I distribute My Paperback Books?

You should distribute your Paperback books everywhere you can within the Paperback book publishing services as this will increase the likelihood of someone buying your Paperback books which will increase your profits.

Should I Create Paperback Books?

You may be put off by creating a Paperback version of your Kindle eBooks after reading what's involved however the written content of your Paperback book has already been created so the majority of the hard work has already been done.

All you have to do is change the formatting of your manuscript, enter your book details, create your Paperback book covers and price your Paperback books which will only take a few hours to do.

Paperback books can also help you earn more and can increase your Amazon rating when bought from Amazon which will increase your Kindle and Paperback book popularity which can result in more Kindle and Paperback book sales and readers.

Also some people prefer to read their books on paper rather than on their computer or iPad or other digital devices they may have and you will be reducing the amount of money you can make from Amazon by only making your books available in a digital format.

Finally Paperback books are excluded from Amazon Select Exclusivity Agreement.

So you can sell your Paperback books on your website or you can list your books on eBay or other marketplaces.

Which is why I recommend that every Kindle eBook you create, publish and market should also have a Paperback version available for your readers to buy.

CREATE AND SELL AN AUDIOBOOK VERSION OF YOUR KINDLE EBOOKS

You can create an Audiobook version of your Kindle eBooks by visiting http://www.acx.com/

Once you have signed to ACX you have a choice of either recording the Audiobooks yourself or you can use one of their narrators to record the Audiobooks for you.

I would recommend you use a narrator to record your Audiobooks as it will take time off your hands and you'll want a professional voice within your recordings.

However whatever method you decide to use is completely up to you.

When you made your decision on how your Audiobooks will be recorded your next step is your distribution agreement.

There are two distribution agreement routes available which are.

The Exclusive Distribution Agreement

If you sign up to the exclusive distribution agreement then your Audiobooks can only be sold on Audible, Amazon, and iTunes.

Your Audiobooks cannot be sold on your website or within any other marketplace.

This includes selling your Audiobooks in CD/DVD format.

You'll receive 40% commission for each sale of your Audiobooks however unless you've recorded the Audiobooks yourself then you'll need to pay the narrator either a 50/50 share of your profits (so you'll receive 20% of the profits) or you'll need to pay onetime fee to the narrator.

The Non Exclusivity Distribution Agreement

The Non Exclusivity Agreement means you can sell your Audiobooks in any marketplace you wish such as your website, eBay and so on.

You can even sell the Audiobooks in a CD Format.

However you will only receive 25% commission for each sale of your Audiobooks on Audible, Amazon, and iTunes and you will have to choose between either recording the Audiobooks yourself or having to pay the narrator a onetime fee to record the Audiobooks for you.

Which Distribution Agreements Do You Recommend I Use?

You should wait and see you see how well the Kindle and Paperback books are selling first before deciding which distribution agreement to choose from.

This way you'll be able to see which distribution agreement is right for you and how your Audiobooks should be created.

For instance if you've published a Kindle eBook and you're making a few sales each month on Amazon then you should choose the exclusivity distribution agreement and you should either record the audiobook yourself or you should share the profits between yourself and the narrator because the onetime fee will probably exceed the profits you'll make from your audiobook and you'll end up losing money.

If however you are making a lot of sales on Amazon and the Paperback books are selling a lot within different marketplaces then you should choose the non-exclusive agreement as your Paperback books are selling well within different marketplaces and you should either record the Audiobooks yourself or pay a narrator a onetime fee to record the audio for you as sharing the profits with the narrator is not an option.

You should also look at your circumstances for instance if you cannot afford to pay a onetime fee to a narrator and you don't want to record the Audiobooks yourself then you will have no choice but to use the exclusivity agreement and to share the profits between yourself and the narrator.

Will I Be Able To Choose How Much Each Audiobook Will Cost?

Unlike your Kindle and Paperback books you do not decide how much to charge your customer if you are selling your Audiobooks on Audible, Amazon, and iTunes.

The price of your Audiobooks is entirely up to them.

However the more pages your Kindle eBooks have the more Audible, Amazon, and iTunes are likely to charge your customer for the sale of your Audiobooks.

Also selling your Audiobooks on Audible, Amazon, and iTunes will increase your Kindle eBooks exposure online and you can charge whatever you like within other marketplaces if you're enrolled in the Non-Exclusivity Agreement.

Should I Create Audiobook Version of My Kindle eBooks?

Creating an audiobook version of your Kindle eBooks is completely up to you but in my opinion it all comes down to whether you're Kindle eBooks are fictional or non-fictional.

If you have created a fictional Kindle eBook then I would

recommend you create an Audiobook when you have either published your second Kindle eBook or you start making a lot of sales from your first Kindle and Paperback book.

This will help you determine whether or not you should share the profits with the narrator or pay the narrator a onetime fee.

For instance If you make a lot of sales and profit from your first Kindle and Paperback book and your profits exceeds the one off cost to the narrator in a big way then you should consider making one off payment to the narrator so you'll be able profit more from the sale of your Audiobooks.

If however you're not making as much as you were hoping for then sharing the profits is the best course of action because you're likely to lose money from the one off payment but you'll still need to create an audiobook version of your Kindle eBook as it can increase your profits and exposure.

Also the majority of fictional Kindle eBooks on Amazon are available as audio and Paperback formats as most fictional Kindle eBook authors want their books to be as accessible as possible.

If however you've created a non-fictional Kindle eBook then creating an audio version of your Kindle eBooks is not essential and should only be created when you have published a vast range of Kindle eBooks.

This is because most non-fictional Audiobooks sell less than fictional Audiobooks do and non-fictional Kindle eBooks are usually less than seventy five pages long so you're unlikely to make a good profit from the sale of your Audiobooks.

The only way you can make a good profit from sale of your non-fictional Audiobooks is by creating and publishing a vast range of non-fictional Audiobooks which will take time.

So I would only recommend you create non-fictional Audiobooks when you have created and published a vast range of non-fictional

Kindle eBooks as you'll be able to slow down the creating, publishing and marketing of your new non fictional Kindle eBooks and you'll be able to use the non-fictional Audiobooks to increase your profits.

I also recommend you share the royalty between you and the narrator as the majority of your non fictional Audiobooks are going to sell less than if you created a series of fictional Kindle eBooks and it will probably be cheaper in the long run to share your profits rather than making a one off payment for each audiobook you've created.

However the choice of how you pay the narrator is completely up to you.

Are There Any Alternative Audiobook Services?

I have a list available at http://dominicbfrost.com/audiobook-publishing-services/ however the best service to use is ACX and it's one I recommend you use.

ENROL IN THE AMAZON KDP SELECT EXCUSIVITY AGREEMENT

Everyone who has created Kindle eBooks should enrol in the KDP Select exclusivity agreement because there are two methods in which you can make money from the exclusivity agreement.

The first method will require no action from you apart from your enrolment into the KDP Select program which will make your Kindle eBooks available to read through Kindle Unlimited and Kindle Owners Lending Library.

You will then be paid based on the share of the KDP Select global fund and how many pages are read from your Kindle eBooks which Amazon can detect through their Kindles software program and the cloud service.

Will This Mean I Will Make Less Money If People Read My Kindle EBooks Through Kindle Unlimited And Kindle Owners Lending Library?

The amount you make from people reading your Kindle eBooks will probably be less than if those readers were to buy your Kindle eBooks.

However if you have published a lot of Kindle eBooks and a lot of pages are read then these pages will add up and you will find that eventually you'll be making a regular passive income from the pages read through the Kindle Unlimited and Kindle Owners Lending Library.

This is why I recommend you join the KDP Select program.

More information on these programs can be found from the links below.

KDP Select
https://kdp.amazon.com/en_US/select?ref_=kdp_BS_D_TN_se

Kindle Unlimited
https://kdp.amazon.com/en_US/help/topic/G201537300

Kindle Owners Lending Library
https://kdp.amazon.com/en_US/help/topic/G201392160

RUN A KINDLE COUNTDOWN DEAL

Running a Kindle countdown deal is the second method you can use to make money from the KDP Select exclusivity agreement.

The Kindle countdown deal will basically allow you to price your Kindle eBooks as low as $0.99 or £0.99 and you'll still earn 70% commission on the sale of your Kindle eBooks for a maximum of seven days after which the price will return to normal.

The Kindle countdown deal also allows you five price increments over a seven day period.

The amount of price increments you'll receive however depends on how much your Kindle eBooks are originally priced as the price increments only increase a dollar or a pound at a time.

So if your Kindle eBooks are priced at $7.99 then you'll have the full five price increments but if your Kindle eBooks are prices at $2.99 you will only get one increment.

Here is an example of how increments can be priced if your Kindle eBooks costs $7.99.

- Day One $0.99
- Day Three $1.99
- Day Five $3.99
- Day Six $4.99
- Day Seven $5.99
- Campaign Ends $7.99

If you have Kindle eBooks priced at $2.99 then you'll only get one increments which is as follows

- Day One to Three $0.99
- Day Four to Seven $1.99

- Campaign Ends $2.99

There will also be a timer next to the price of your Kindle eBooks showing how long the visitor has to buy your Kindle eBooks before the price increases or returns to normal which creates urgency for the visitor to buy your Kindle eBooks before the price goes up.

However you could price your Kindle eBooks at $0.99 or another lower for the full seven days instead of using price increments which may increase the amount of sales you make from your Kindle eBooks but you may also decrease the amount of money you could have made.

You should also consider pricing your Paperback books to around $12.99 or higher as the Kindle countdown deal doesn't show the savings made from your Kindle eBooks but the savings made if they bought your Paperback books.

So let's say your Kindle eBooks are priced at $7.99 and the Paperback books are priced at $12.99.

The countdown deal is $0.99 the buyer will see the original print price of $12.99 not the original price of your Kindle eBooks. which is $7.99 and they'll see they will save $12.00 if they buy within a certain amount of time and will also see that they will save 93% of the cost of your Kindle eBooks which entices the reader to want to buy your Kindle eBooks even more.

So to sum it up if your Kindle eBooks are priced higher you'll receive more price increments and if your Paperback books are priced higher the reader will think they're making a huge saving so they're more likely to buy them due to the urgency of the Kindle eBooks getting higher in price as every day goes by.

How Do I Run a Kindle Countdown Deal?

In order to run a Kindle countdown deal you will firstly need to sign into your Kindle account at https://kdp.amazon.com then select the promote and advertise button next to the Kindle eBook you want to run the Kindle countdown deal on.

You'll then need to select the Kindle countdown deal radio button and select create a new Kindle countdown deal button.

You'll need to decide the marketplace which can only be run at either Amazon.com or Amazon.co.uk and you'll then need to select start and end dates with a maximum of 7 days.

Finally you'll need to select the number of price increments and the starting list price.

What Are the Conditions of Running a Kindle Countdown Deal?

One of the main conditions is that you cannot change the price of your Kindle eBooks for thirty days if it's changed it won't let you enrol into Kindle countdown deal for another thirty days.

You also can't change the price of your Kindle eBooks after the Kindle countdown deal ends for fourteen days and you can only run one Kindle countdown deal per Kindle Select term which runs every ninety days.

Finally if you use the free Kindle promotional you will be ineligible for the Kindle countdown deal.

More Information can be found at
https://kdp.amazon.com/en_US/help/topic/G201298280.

Should I Run A Kindle Countdown Deal?

I only recommend you run a Kindle countdown deal if your Kindle eBooks have a lot of reviews and sales, you published a Paperback version of your Kindle eBooks and your Kindle eBooks is priced high within the last thirty days.

I do not recommend you use the Kindle countdown deal if you have just released your Kindle eBooks within the last thirty days as you will have no reason to justify the hike in price of your Kindle/Paperback books and you're unlikely to have any review so you're unlikely to get anyone buying your newly released Kindle eBooks even if you took part in the Kindle countdown deal.

If you have just released your Kindle eBooks then I recommend you sell your Kindle eBooks at a price of $2.99 without using countdown deals.

SELL THE FILM AND TELEVISION RIGHTS TO YOUR KINDLE EBOOKS

Every fictional Kindle eBook writer should try and sell the film and television rights to their Kindle eBooks as not only will you be able to make more money but it may give you the chance to see your Kindle eBooks being turned into a film or television show.

What Should I Do First?

The first thing you should do is create, publish and market your Kindle/Paperback books on Amazon and get as many buyers, readers and five star reviews as you can.

By doing this you will have a much better chance of getting your Kindle/Paperback books noticed by directors, producers and production/studio companies as they'll be able to see from your Kindle eBook web page your book rating, your five star reviews and the amount of fans who will love to watch a film and television adaption of your Kindle eBooks.

A director, producer or production/studio company will be interested in the information because a usual film or television show from a Screenplay read by only a few select people within the film and television industry will not know whether they've made a hit until it's been broadcast.

So if the reviews are bad and people decide not to watch the film or television show then it means they'll lose out on a lot of money and they're a lot of film and television shows which flop.

However because you've published a Kindle and Paperback version of your books and you've got a lot of sales, readers and fans who have given you five star reviews then the directors, producers and production/studio companies will already know the audience will love the film or television adaption of your Kindle eBooks before it's even been broadcast.

Which is why your Kindle eBooks will stand out from the other books and Screenplays the directors, producers and production/studio companies are given.

If you're very lucky you may even be contacted by directors, producers or production/studio companies before you decide to pitch your Kindle eBooks to them.

Having your Kindle/Paperback books published first before sending them to production/studio companies can also prove that you have the rights to the storyline.

Convert Your Kindle eBooks into Screenplays

Converting your Kindle eBooks into Screenplays isn't essential but should be done in order to increase your chances of selling the film and television rights because some directors, producers and production/studio companies will only want to read Screenplays.

Also a director, producer and production/studio company will need to hire someone in order to convert your Kindle eBooks into Screenplays which will cost them money.

So by converting your Kindle eBooks into Screenplays you will be increasing your Kindle eBooks visibility to the directors, producers and production/studio companies and you'll be saving them money.

You'll also increase your credibility if you send them your Kindle and Paperback books together with your Screenplays for them to read.

The format of a Screenplay is shown at https://www.writersstore.com/how-to-write-a-screenplay-a-guide-to-scriptwriting/

You can also use the following programs listed on my website at http://dominicbfrost.com/screenwriting-software/ in order to create your own Screenplays or you can visit http://dominicbfrost.com/freelance-job-posting-and-hiring-websites/ where you can hire someone to convert your Kindle eBooks into Screenplays.

However Screenwriters will charge a lot of money for this so it's probably best to convert your Kindle eBooks into Screenplays yourself.

Finally once the director, producer and production/studio company has bought the film and television rights to your Kindle eBooks then they're under no obligation to use your Screenplays.

However that's the film and television business for you.

Marketing and Submitting Your Kindle/Paperback Books and Screenplays

There are different ways you can market and submit your books and Screenplays to directors, producers, production/studio companies and anyone else within the film and television industry.

The following pages will show you the methods you can use but there is no right or wrong way to do this as long as you keep trying no matter how frustrated you may get.

Submit Your Books and Screenplays to Production and Studio Companies

Submitting your books and Screenplays to production/studio companies is one of the most frequently used method you can use it sometimes works.

You should firstly find and research as many film and television production and studio companies as you can and see what sort of film and television shows they create.

Make a list of the top of the top film and television production and studio companies within your genre and their submission guidelines.

I have a list of film and television production/ studio companies at http://dominicbfrost.com/film-and-television-production-studio-companies/.

You'll then need to create a query letters which will basically outlining your storylines in a one or two sentence letter along with the reasons why they should be interested in buying the film and television rights to your Kindle eBooks such as your five star reviews and your Kindle eBook rating.
You should also include your Kindle eBook web page links within the query letter so they can see for themselves the ratings and reviews you have received from your Kindle eBooks.

Samples of query letters can be found at https://virtualpitchfest.com/how-it-works/sample-query-letters/.

You should then send your query letter to every production and studio company within your list along with a free copies of your books and Screenplay (if requested on the production/studio company website).

You should keep doing this regularly every six months to a year to the same or new production and studio companies as this will increase the chances of getting your Kindle eBooks noticed.

Just make sure that your Kindle/Paperback eBooks are published first before submitting them your Screenplay as this forms as proof that you have the rights to the storyline.

If you do not do this then some production/studio companies may consider trying to steal your Screenplay and turning it into a film/television show without any contract/agreement.

Finally you should only stop sending them your query letters, Kindle eBooks, Paperback books and Screenplays when the film and television rights are sold or the production/studio company sends you a rejection letter/email.

Ignore the "No Unsolicited Material" Message on the Producer/Studio Company Website.

When visiting the production and studio company websites you may see a message which basically says that they will not accept any unsolicited material.

You should immediately ignore this message and send them your query letter as the worst thing they will do is throw it away and really it's their loss if they do.

It all comes down to timing as you may catch them at a good time and they may decide to read your query letter which interests them so they decide to read your books and ask for a copy of your Screenplay anyway.

A Quick Note about Sending Your Kindle eBooks via Email

If you are enrolled in the KDP Select exclusivity program then the digital version of your books can only be sold or given away via Amazon and nowhere else.

However the KDP Select exclusivity program does allow you to send a free professional reviewer version of your Kindle eBooks via email for the purpose of editing, proofreading and helping with other quality improvements.

So you are allowed to send the digital version of your Kindle eBooks and Screenplays to production and studio companies via email.

You're also allowed to send the digital version of your books via email to directors and producers but I'd be careful with sending your digital books to anyone else as you do not want to violate the KDP Select exclusivity agreement.

So limit sending your Kindle eBooks via email to directors, producers and production/studio companies only.

If however you're concerned about this then you can send them your Paperback books instead of sending them your Kindle eBook via email.

You can also stop the renewal of your Kindle eBook from the KDP Select Enrolment so that when it expires you can send them free copies of your Kindle eBooks to anyone you want via email or by any other means.

What's The Process after Submission?

Your query letters, books and your Screenplays will firstly be sent to gatekeepers (also known as readers).

The Gatekeepers will then decide whether it's worth giving your books and Screenplays to the directors/producer.

Getting Pass the Gatekeepers

If you're lucky then either one or many of your books and Screenplays has interested the gatekeepers and they will be sent to a director, producer who'll make the decision as to whether or not to buy the film or television rights.

However because of the volume of books and Screenplays the gatekeepers receive it's unlikely that they'll read them all.

They'll probably just read the synopsis or the first few pages of your books and Screenplays and decide whether or not to chuck the material away.

They may even in some cases take one stack of query letters, books and Screenplays and chuck them away without reading them and take another stack and choose their top ten and bin the rest.

It's very much like sending a C.V. they're not going to go through each one as it will take too long.

How to Get Your Kindle/Paperback Book and Screenplay Noticed By the Gatekeepers

The best way to get your books and Screenplays noticed by the gatekeepers is to firstly find out who they are and then socialize with them at festivals and events and try and be as nice and friendly to them as you can.

However this will only help in getting your books and Screenplays noticed and possibly read by the gatekeepers.

It does not guarantee that they will send your books and Screenplays to a directors or producer.

This is because the gatekeepers' job will be on the line if the director or producer continually receives books and Screenplays which they're not interested in.

So if the gatekeeper doesn't like the books and Screenplays you send them then no matter how friendly and nice you are to them they'll still bin the material and move on.

Submit Your Screenplay to Contests

This is basically the same route you take with sending your Screenplay to production and studio companies however you won't need to send them your Kindle/ Paperback books and even in some cases your query letters.

You will however need to send them your contact information; your Screenplay and in some cases a small fee.

However if you win the contest you will not be selling the film and television rights to your Kindle eBooks.

You will instead receive a cash or gift prize which could be anything from Screenplay coaching or even a holiday.

Your Screenplay will also be more noticeable to film and television professional within the industry even if you don't win the contest in some cases.

Some of the Screenplay contests such as the ones listed on my website at http://dominicbfrost.com/screenwriting-contests/ are genuinely contests you should consider applying for.

However some aren't and some are contests which are either only interested in taking your money or are only interested in stealing your Screenplay.

So before applying to a Screenplay contest you should do your research and check out the people who are judging the Screenplays and see if they're within the film and television industry.

Get Yourself a Literature/Screenwriter Agent

Getting a Literature/Screenwriter agent will help you market you books and Screenplays to film and television production companies and will help you when it comes to selling the rights to your Kindle eBooks as they'll be making about 10% from the sale of the rights.

They'll also know a lot of people within the film and television industry and can send your books and Screenplays to a lot of important people within the industry.

However there is a problem which is getting a Literature/Screenwriter agent to work for you can be even harder than getting a production/studio company to read your books and Screenplays as you'll need to send the Literature/Screenwriter a your C.V. with film or television references.

They'll then decide whether they want to represent you and it's unlikely they will unless they either love your books and Screenplays or you've got a lot of experience within writing and film making.

However although having a Literature/Screenwriter agent will help you get your books and Screenplays noticed by directors, producers and production/studio companies it's not essential.

Maybe later when you sell the film and television rights to some of your Kindle eBooks you can look at getting yourself a Literature/Screenwriter agent but I wouldn't look at getting yourself an agent if this is your first book and Screenplay you're submitting.

Pitch Your Kindle eBooks at Film and Television Festivals and Events

Going to film and television festivals and events is the best way to market your Kindle eBooks as being successful in the film and television industry is not about what you know or what you have it's who you know and by regularly going to these festivals and events will increase the amount of people you'll know and will give you the chance to pitch your Kindle eBooks to them.

However before you go to these events this you will need to do the following.

Work On Your Pitching Skills

You need to pitch your Kindle eBooks as best as you can and the best way to do this is to practice. The pitch shouldn't be too long and should attract the people at the event to general storyline of your Kindle eBooks.

You should also mention how many buyers and reviews your Kindle eBooks have received which will make your Kindle eBook stand out.

Look Presentable

You need to clean yourself up and look presentable so that you can show to people within the film and television industry that you are serious about marketing your Kindle eBooks.

You should also consider wearing something that will help them remember who you are such as a tie or hat or something that make you stand out from the crowd.

Have Business Cards Ready to Hand Out

You should have business cards ready to hand out to everyone you talk to at the film and television festivals and events so that they know how to contact you after the festival/event.

Each business card will need to have the following Information.

- Your name
- Email address
- Phone number
- Website
- Kindle eBook Titles

You can also include a link to the Kindle eBooks you want to market.

If you haven't created and printed a business card yet then you can use the following services from http://dominicbfrost.com/business-cards/ to create a few of them but remember you'll need a lot of business cards as your goal will not only to pitch your Kindle eBooks but to also hand out as many business cards as you can.

Bring Some Money with You

This is a place to socialize so you'll need money to buy a few drinks and have some fun while you're there and you can't do this unless you have some money available to spend.

Find Out Time, Location and Entry Requirements

There are many film and television festivals and events but sometimes the time and place may not be appropriate for you to attend or it's too far or it's at a time you cannot attend so you'll need to find out when and where these festivals and events take place.

You may also not be allowed to go to the festival or event unless you have a ticket which may either be free, cost money or only be available by invitation only so check the entry requirements first.

Once At the Festival or Event

When you are at the festival or event you should then meet and socialize with everyone you can, ask them what they're working on and ask a few questions and answer a few questions they ask from you then subtly pitch your Kindle eBooks to them.

Finally before you move onto talking to someone else you should hand them your business cards and hopefully they'll hand you their business cards as well which you can use to contact them a few days later after the festival or event.

When you do contact them either via email, phone call or by other means you should firstly remind them who you are by mentioning the distinguishable clothing you were wearing or the conversation you were having with them at the festival/event.

You should then try and pitch your Kindle eBooks to them again one more time.

You should also not be put off if they're an actor or runner as they mention your Kindle eBooks to other people and word of mouth can spread from a runner to a producer very quickly so talk to them and market your Kindle eBooks to everyone you can at the festivals and events.

Never Act Inappropriately

One more thing which you should never do is act inappropriately for instance having a few drinks is OK but getting drunk and disorderly is really bad and could get you banned from any more festivals and events they may have.

You also shouldn't swear, be rude or argue with anyone.

In General What Should You Do At The Festival And Event?

In general you'll need to have fun, socialize, pitch your Kindle eBooks, hand out your business cards and collect as many business cards as you can so that you can remind them about your Kindle eBooks later on after the festival/event.

Get Your Kindle eBook Fans to Appeal to the Production/Studio Companies

Your Kindle eBook readers and fans could help you sell the film and television rights to the Production/Studio companies.

All you have to do is mention on your website and social media accounts that you're trying to turn your Kindle eBooks into a film or television show and would appreciate it if they can contact some of the production/studio companies you've been pitching to and try and convince them to buy the film and television rights to your Kindle eBooks.

The production/studio companies will hopefully be inundated with emails, tweets and messages from your readers and fans appealing to them to buy the film and television rights to your Kindle eBooks which the production/studio companies will find hard to ignore.

You can even attach your message to a memorable hashtag such as

#turnitintoamovie #booktomovie, #booktofilm #turnbooktitleintoamovie and so on.

Market Your Kindle/Paperback Books to As Many People within the Film and Television Industry as You Can

The film and television industry is all about who you know not what you know and as previously mentioned so you should market your Kindle/Paperback books to everyone within the film and television industry no matter what position they hold because they may eventually meet up and talk with other major directors and producers within the film and television industry.

These people may even start to read your Kindle/Paperback books in their spare time which may catch the directors or producers eye so you should market your Kindle/Paperback books to everyone within the film and television industry.

In order to do market your Kindle/Paperback books to everyone in the film and television industry you can as previously mentioned go to film and television festivals and events and pitch your Kindle eBooks and give them your business cards.

However you will find that not everyone within the film and television industry will be at the same festival and events you go to.

So you'll need search online for people within the industry by using social media accounts such as Twitter, Facebook, LinkedIn and you can find people within the IMDB database at http://www.imdb.com/ which is a really good service you can use.

You can also find out who else works for a production/studio companies you've sent your books and Screenplays to by visiting the companies web address or by searching on LinkedIn and look through all their other social media accounts.

How Do You Market Your Kindle/Paperback Books to These People Online?

I go over how you can market your Kindle/Paperback books within my [Kindle Marketing Victory](#) book which I recommend you read but you should try and follow, like subscribe to all of their social media accounts.

You should also send them a tweet or a direct message on Twitter, Instagram, YouTube and LinkedIn telling them about your Kindle/Paperback Books.

Do Not Send Them a Free Copy of Your Kindle eBook via Email

If you are enrolled into the KDP Select program then as mentioned before unless you're submitting your Kindle eBooks to directors, producers or a production/studio companies then you cannot send them a free copy of your Kindle eBooks via email.

However you do have five free promotional days at your disposal you can use.

So you could just send them two private messages before your free Kindle promotion begins and let them know when your Kindle eBooks will be free to download and another two private messages when your Kindle eBooks are available for free.

This will increase the amount of free Kindle eBook downloads.

You can also let them know when you're running a Kindle countdown deal which will increase the profits you make.

Leaving Your Paperback Books at Convenient Places for Staff within Production/Studio Company to Read

Leaving your Paperback books at convenient place for staff within the production/studio company to find and read is another way to get your books noticed as staff members may start to talk about your Paperback books to directors/producers which may lead to them reading your Paperback books to.

All you have to do is leave your Paperback books at locations such as the reception area or a desk at a production/studio company or if you know a lot of the staff sit at a particular time and a particular table in a coffee shop, or café you could leave your Paperback books on the table before they arrive for them to read.

Selling the Film and Television Rights to Your Kindle eBooks

If you've created some really good Kindle eBooks and you have followed the steps within this chapter then you'll hopefully find a production/studio company who will want to buy the film and television rights to your Kindle eBooks.

If this occurs then you'll need to get yourself a Literature/Screenplay agent or you'll need a legal representative to help you negotiate the terms of the contract.

I would recommend a solicitor within the business but don't use someone they recommend as they're most likely be working for the production/studio company and not you.

This will be bad as the film and television industry is full of people and companies who will want to take advantage of you and you could end up signing a contract which benefits the production/studio more than you and leaves you with a bad deal.

So get an impartial solicitor who you trust and who hasn't worked for the production/studio company before.

Two Main Parts of the Contract

Usually there are two main parts of the contract which are.

1. The option which will take the movie or television rights of your Kindle eBooks off the market.
2. The purchase price which will be the cost of turning your Kindle eBooks into a movie or television series.

The option stage is taking the film and television rights off the market so if another production company wants to buy the rights to your Kindle eBooks then you'll be unable to do so as you've already signed the contract with another film production/studio company.

The amount you will receive to take the film and television rights off the market can be as little as one dollar to a few thousand dollars.

The option stage should also have an expiry date which means that if they don't progress to the purchase price and turn your Kindle eBooks into a film or television show within a certain period of time then the film and television rights will be available on the market again for another production/studio company to buy.

You will need to try and keep the expiry date as short as possible whereas the production/studio company will want to keep the rights for as long as possible.

You should try to keep the rights in between six to nine months.

Anything over eighteen months is too long and should not be signed as the director, producer or production/studio company may only want the rights so that another director, producer or production/studio company doesn't get the rights to your Kindle eBooks and they may have no intention of turning your Kindle eBooks into a film or television show.

You should also in the contract stipulate that they can buy the rights again when the option expires if they need more time however you or they are under no obligation to do so.

The purchase price stage is when production/studio company intends to turn your Kindle eBooks into a film or television show this will usually occur when they have setup the film/television budget they've chosen which actors are going to star in film/television show and they intend to start filming soon.

If your Kindle eBooks get this stage then you should state in the contract that you want a percentage of the budget and not a specific cash amount.

The reason why you shouldn't set a specific amount and this is because the budget can either be small or very, very large and you may end up losing out on a lot of money just by stating you want a specific amount.

For instance small film production companies are bought by bigger film studio companies all the time and the bigger film studio companies will have a lot more money to spend on the budget of a film or television show.

So if the small film production company was bought by a big studio company and they decides to turn your Kindle eBooks into a big film or television show then you will have lost out on a lot of money if the purchase price of your Kindle eBooks was set at a very small specific price.

It's much better to set the purchase price to a variable amount based on the budget of the film or television show.

You'll want to keep it to around 1% to 3% of the budget and no more.

You'll also need to cap the purchase price as the production/studio company don't want the purchase price to be unlimited so it should have a limit of around two to five million dollars.

Other Rights

You should look at some of the other rights you might be signing to the production/studio company.

For instance they may be able to create a spin off version of your Kindle eBooks and will they may be able to change the ending of your Kindle eBooks within the film or television show.

So you need to be clear on what you are unwilling to compromise on to your agent or solicitor but not the production/studio company.

If the deal the production/studio company is offering to you is lower than you were hoping then you should think it over before deciding whether it's worth selling the film or television rights or whether it will be better to look for another production/studio company.

Why Should I Sell the Film and Television Rights to My Kindle eBooks?

Firstly as stated in the contract you will receive payment for taking the rights off the market and you'll receive another larger payment if your Kindle eBooks are turned into a film or television show.

If it gets to this stage and the film and television show is very popular then this will increase the exposure of your Kindle eBooks online and you will see an increase in sales of your Kindle eBooks and the amount of readers you have.

You could also see your Kindle eBooks being turned into a film or television show which is very rewarding.

How likely After the Option Stage Will My Kindle eBooks be turned into a Film or Television Show?

The majority of the books and Screenplays that reaches the option stage will never actually get turned into a film or television show.

The reason for this is because the director, producer or

production/studio company has probably got a lot of books and Screenplays they have optioned and the chances of your Kindle eBooks being turned into a film or television show depends on a lot of factors such as money, actors, location, availability and so on.

However getting to the option stage is a big step forward in turning your Kindle eBooks into a film or television show.

Should I Bother Selling the Film and Television Rights to My Kindle eBooks?

You should try your best to sell the film and television rights to your Kindle eBook as you will receive more money and will gain more exposure to your Kindle eBooks.

Also you have nothing to lose.

What Should You Do If I Can't Get Any Production/Studio Company to Buy the Film and Television Rights to My Kindle eBooks?

If you can't sell the film and television rights either because the deal they're offering to you is rubbish or no production/studio company is interested in buying the film and television rights to your Kindle eBooks then you shouldn't give up no matter how frustrated you get.

Keep marketing and sending copies of your books and Screenplays to as many production/studio companies as you can and try to find new production/studio company who will be willing to buy the film and television rights to your Kindle eBooks.

You can also still make money selling your Kindle/Paperback books and you can use some of the other techniques within my Kindle Money Making Victory book to make some more money.

You should also keep making more Kindle eBooks and hopefully one of them will be more successful than the last.

What Do You Recommend I Do?

My advice is to keep creating, publishing, marketing and pitching your Kindle eBooks to people within the film and television industry and try and get more reviews, readers and buyers as the more you get the more of a chance of you being able to sell the film and television rights to your Kindle eBooks and never give up no matter how frustrated you get.

USING YOUR WEBSITE TO MAKE MONEY FROM YOUR KINDLE EBOOKS

Every Kindle eBook author needs a website because it's a great way to promote and make money from your Kindle eBooks.

In order to create a website you will need a domain name which could be as simple as your author/pen name or the title of your Kindle eBook series or even a name which resembles the topic your Kindle eBooks are about.

When you have come up with a name you'll then need to find out whether it's available to buy

You can do this by visiting one of the domain registration services which I have listed within my website at http://dominicbfrost.com/domain-name-registration-services/

You should also only buy a domain name with the preferred .com extension rather than the other extensions available as it's the most popular and well known extension to use.

Once you bought a domain name you'll then need to buy web hosting in order to store all of you website files.

I have a list of popular web hosting providers on my website at http://dominicbfrost.com/web-hosting-services/.

You'll also find most domain registrars offer web hosting to.

Once you have your domain name and web hosting you'll then need to design the website and add content

I recommend you use a free blogging tool such as WordPress which can be easily installed, has a selection of free website templates you can use and has a very simple interface which will allow you to add the necessary content onto your website.

Once you have your website all setup you'll then need to add your website link within your Kindle eBooks.

My [Kindle Marketing Victory](#) book will show you where you should add your website links within your Kindle eBooks but it's essential that you do this as some readers will click on your website link and be redirected to your website where you will be able to make some more money from those visitors and within the next few chapters I will be showing you how you can do this.

I also recommend you add analytical service such as [Google Analytics](#) or [Statcounter](#) within your website so that you can gather more information on your website visitors and where they came from as they may not all come from your Kindle eBooks but also from Google, social media accounts and so on.

You can also find out which web pages within your website are popular than others.

Finally you should add legal information such as disclaimers, privacy and so on within your website to prevent any legal issues that may occur.

More information about what legal information you should add onto your website can be found at http://dominicbfrost.com/legal-information-to-add-onto-your-website/.

What Content Should I Never Add Within My Website?

You should never add any illegal; hate or pornographic content within your website as this will be against Amazons terms of service and your Kindle eBooks will be taken off Amazon and you may find yourself in legal trouble.

PROMOTE YOUR KINDLE EBOOKS ON YOUR WEBSITE

This is the most obvious way to make money from your website because the majority of your website visitors will want to know more about some of the Kindle eBooks you're published.

So you'll need to add some promotional content such as information about your Kindle eBooks, images, banners, videos and so on in the hopes that they will visit your Amazon book pages and buy your Kindle eBooks.

You should also read the chapter about affiliate marketing as this is another way your website visitors can make you money if they visit your Amazon book pages from your website and not just from the sale of your Kindle eBooks.

Do You Recommend I Promote My Kindle eBooks from My Website?

Yes you should promote your Kindle eBooks on your website as you'll be increasing the amount of Kindle eBook sales and money you make.

CREATE AND SELL YOUR OWN MERCHANDIZE ON YOUR WEBSITE

Creating and selling your own merchandize is another great way to make money from your website.

You can create and sell books, video tutorials, music, software, CD's, DVD's, t-shirts, posters, toys and more.

To sell merchandize on your website you will need to do the following.

1. Create the merchandize.
2. Add the merchandize onto your website.
3. Setup a payment processor to handle payments from your customers.
4. Package and post the merchandize to your customers.

This may put you off but there are tools and services which can help.

For instance if you intend to create and sell t shirts and posters then you can use services such as https://www.cafepress.com or https://www.spreadshirt.com which will create the merchandize for you and take care of packaging posting and payments of the merchandize from your customers.

All you have to do is create and upload a unique design for your merchandize, decide how much you want to charge and profit from the sale of your merchandize and add their product onto your website.

If you're selling digital merchandize such as eBooks, video, audio, images, software and so on then all you need to do is create the digital merchandize, upload it somewhere secure on your website, add the digital merchandize onto your website and have a payment processor which will redirect them to your digital product after payment is received.

There are a lot of payment processors to choose from such as PayPal, Clickbank, 2Checkout and so on.

I also have of other payment processor service available for you to use on my website at http://dominicbfrost.com/payment-processors/

What Merchandize Should I Sell?

You should sell merchandize related to your Kindle eBooks.

For instance if you created a series of fictional Kindle eBooks then you could use services such as Cafepress and Spreadshirt to create and sell posters and clothing with your Kindle eBook cover images included within merchandize designs.

You can also sell exclusive eBooks which will only be sold on your website and nowhere else.

If however you've created a series of non-fictional Kindle eBooks then you could sell digital merchandize that gives people more information a topic related to your Kindle eBooks.

So if you've created Kindle eBooks about investing then you could create a video or unique eBook about investing.

Does All of the Merchandize Have To Be Sold On My Website?

No

In fact it might be better if you not only sell your merchandize on your website but you also sell your merchandize at other marketplaces and let your website visitors know about the other marketplaces your selling your merchandize from which will increase the amount of sales you make.

I have a list of other marketplaces you can use and what you can use to sell on them at http://dominicbfrost.com/online-marketplaces/.

You will however need to pay to list and/or sell your merchandize within other marketplace.

But your merchandize will be more accessible.

Do You Recommend I Sell My Own Merchandize on My Website?

It depends on what type of Kindle eBooks you've created.

If you've created a series of fictional Kindle eBooks then I'd recommend you use Cafepress and Spreadshirt to create merchandize to sell onto your website as it will take very little time to create, add and sell the merchandize onto your website.

The merchandize will also promote your fictional Kindle eBooks which will make you some extra money.

You should also look at creating an exclusive eBook only sold on your website but only when your Kindle eBooks are more popular on Amazon.

If however you've created a series of non-fictional Kindle eBooks then people will not want clothing or posters on topics you've written about.

They will however be interested in buying another eBook, video or other digital merchandize within the topic you've written which will take a lot of time to create.

So it might be better to look at using one of the other methods within my Kindle Money Making Victory book to make money from your Kindle eBooks such as Affiliate Marketing and then maybe look at creating your own digital merchandize later on when you've created a full range of Kindle eBooks and have some time on your hands.

PROVIDE AND SELL A SERVICE ON YOUR WEBSITE

Providing and selling a services is another option you can take in order to make money from your website.

The service you provide needs to be compatible with the Kindle eBooks you've created so if you've created a series of Kindle eBooks about creating a website then you can provide a web hosting service on your website.

What Are the Best Services Compatible with Kindle eBooks?

The best services you can provide to people who read your Kindle eBooks and visit your website are digital services such as.

- Web hosting
- Web design
- Internet marketing
- Book writing
- Software engineering
- Graphic designing
- Video creation

The list goes on.

Specialist services such as therapy, hypnotherapy, business consulting are also compatible with Kindle eBook.

However you must be qualified to provide these service and know what you're doing otherwise word will spread and you will start to get bad reviews.

Why are these services compatible with the Kindle eBooks I can sell?

Digital service are compatible with the Kindle eBooks you sell as these services can be provided, sold and delivered to people worldwide without having to travel to and from your customers location.

Specialist services are also compatible with the Kindle eBooks you sell because people who want these services will either be willing to travel to you or are willing to pay your travel expenses for you to travel them

However again you must be qualified to provide these service and know what you're doing otherwise word will spread and you will start to get bad reviews.

What Services Aren't Compatible with Kindle eBooks?

Services which you can only provide locally and aren't specialist services or services which are highly saturated are the worst type of services which are not compatible with Kindle eBooks.

However this doesn't mean you can't use your Kindle eBooks to provide these services and you may be able to use your Kindle eBooks to branch out into other areas worldwide.

Are There Other Ways I Can Use My Services?

You could turn your service into a product to sell onto your website instead.

For instance if you're a web designer you can create web design templates and sell them on your website or if you're a hypnotherapist then you can sell video and audio recordings on how to quit smoking or something similar.

Do You Recommend I Sell My Services on My Website?

Unless you're already running a business or are working within the service industry and have the time to either provide these services or have a team of people who can provide these services for you then I wouldn't use this method as it's a lot of work and will take a lot of time and energy to run.

However it's still a good way to make money which you may be able to explore if you wanted to.

CREATE AND SELL A MEMBERSHIP SERVICE ON YOUR WEBSITE

Creating and selling a membership service is very similar to creating and selling digital merchandize.

The big difference however is that people will need to become members to your service in order to access the digital content you are providing and if you are creating a paid membership service then you'll need to create a lot of digital merchandize for your members.

So in a way you are turning your content and digital merchandize into a service which you are providing to your customers.

Free Membership Services

The best free membership service which I recommend everyone create and use is an email newsletter service.

It's very simple to create and can be used to not only provide useful information and advice to your members but you can also use it to market your website, your new and existing Kindle eBooks and other methods you are using to make money from your Kindle eBooks.

However I am not going to go into detail about creating this type of membership service as it's mostly used for marketing purposes.

If you want to learn more about how you can create and use an email newsletter service then please read the Create An Email Newsletter chapter of my Kindle Marketing Victory book.

There are also some other free membership services you can provide such as forums which .are great if you want people to communicate with you and others within the forum.

You'll need to moderate the forum yourself and assign moderators you trust to help you make sure all members within the forum comply with your forum rules.

However creating a free forum isn't essential as people mostly use social media websites rather than forums to communicate to you and others interested in your Kindle eBooks.

You can use one of the programs I've listed on my website at http://dominicbfrost.com/forum-software/ in order to create a forum for you to use on your website.

Paid Membership Service

The best way you can create a paid membership service is by using a membership software program which will create restricted area on your website for members only.

I have a list of membership software programs you can use on my website at http://dominicbfrost.com/membership-software-programs/.

You will then have control over what content and material members can see.

You can also create a paid membership service using one of the email autoresponder services which I have a list use on my website at http://dominicbfrost.com/email-autoresponder-services/.

However I recommend you use one of the membership software programs at http://dominicbfrost.com/membership-software-programs/ rather than an email autoresponder service as people prefer to log into a website for new content rather than having to check their email for the content to be available.

How Do I Make Money from a Paid Membership Service?

In order for you to make money from your paid membership service you'll need to not only try and sell your paid membership service to your website visitors but you'll also need to provide and maintain a good service for your members so that they will stay loyal, remain members and can continually send you daily, weekly, monthly and yearly payments.

What's The Best Type of Membership Service You Can Provide Your Paid Members?

The best type of membership service you can provide is an online training courses related to the Kindle eBooks you've created.

So if you've created a series of Kindle eBooks about golf then you should look at giving your members an online video course about how to play golf.

What Kind of Content Should I Provide To My Paid Members?

You can provide video, audio, eBooks, images, webinars and so on.

However you should avoid anything software related as it does take a lot of expertise, time and money to create unless you're good at creating software and updating the software.

What Content Restrictions Should I Give To My Members?

This is all determined by how much content you have and how much they're willing to pay in advance for your content.

You could technically give out all of the content to every paid member without any restrictions.

However if you only created twelve videos which are thirty minutes in length then offering all of the content to every paid member is not fair for the members who paid for a yearly or lifetime membership service as they'll eventually find out they could have got all the content they needed for a highly discounted price if they paid for the daily, weekly or monthly membership service.

The best way to set it up in the above example would be to create a daily, weekly and monthly member service get rid of the yearly and lifetime service and provide your members with one video a week.

By doing this they'll feel like getting a lot of content from the membership program in a short space of time.

If however you have a lot of video and written content which lasts for a lot of time which is only accessible through your website then you could provide full access to all of your members within your paid membership service.

However it's probably best that if a member has signed up for a daily, weekly, monthly membership service that you should give them the content gradually each day, week or month to help keep your members loyal to your membership service.

You should also offer your yearly members more immediate content since they paid more in advance for access to the content within your membership service.

How Long Should The Membership Service Last For?

It depends on the amount of content you have and the frequency of the content you want to give your members.

For instance if you only have twelve videos then if you offer the video's on a weekly basis then you can offer a weekly or a monthly membership service lasting for three months.

Yet if you offer the same video on a monthly basis then you can either offer a monthly or a full membership service.

However I'd recommend you create a lot more content than just twelve video's if you want to run the membership service for a year or longer.

You can also continually create content so that your membership service can be extended for your members want more content.

However you'll need to spend some of your time and work in order to create the extra content for your membership service.

Lifetime membership is probably a membership you want to avoid, especially if you have created a limited amount of content to give to your members.

It should only be used if you have regular information which you can easily create and can provide for a lifetime such as stock tips, tipster service and so on.

How Much Should I Charge My Members To Join My Membership Service?

The amount you charge your members to join your membership service is completely up to you.

However you should offer a discount to members who pay in advance for your yearly membership service.

For instance if you charge $20 to become a member of a paid service then over the course of a year they will have paid $240 a year

So I would recommend you charge your members $200 for your yearly membership and advertise the fact that they'll save $40 if they sign up to your yearly membership service.

This will lead to more people signing up to your yearly membership service.

However again the amount you charge your members to join your membership service is completely up to you

Do You Recommend I Create a Free Membership Service?

I recommend that every Kindle eBook author creates a free email newsletter service as it can be used as a marketing tool which will help you make money from the methods shown within this book.

You can also create a free forum membership service if you want but people mostly use social media to communicate to you and other people about Kindle eBooks and other topics.

So you're unlikely to get many members signing up to the forum unless your Kindle eBooks are very popular.

Do You Recommend I Create a Paid Membership Service?

If you've created a series of fictional Kindle eBooks then I don't recommend you create a paid membership service at all because the only thing you can provide to your members is your Kindle eBooks and people would rather buy them on Amazon.

You'll also be unable to provide your Kindle eBooks as part of your membership program if you've enrolled in the KDP Select Exclusivity Agreement.

If however you've created a series of non-fictional Kindle eBooks then you could create a membership service about a topic related to your non fictional Kindle eBooks

But although providing a paid membership services is incredibly profitable you will still need to create a lot content which will take a lot of time and work off your hands.

In my opinion you should only consider creating a paid membership service when you've created a vast range of non-fictional Kindle eBooks and have time on your hands to create the paid membership service.

Until then you should focus on some of the other methods you can use to make money from your Kindle eBooks.

USE A DROP SHIPPING SERVICE TO SELL PRODUCTS ON YOUR WEBSITE

Drop shipping is a method in which you can make money from other people's products.

To do this you will firstly need to find and sign up to a drop shipping service.

You'll then need to list some of the products available on the drop shipping service onto your website at a higher price the drop shipper service is selling them for so you can make a profit.

You'll also need to look at other costs the drop shipper will charge you for such as the cost of postage and packaging, vat, tax and so on and you should look at how much the payment processors will charge you for each payment the customer makes which you'll also need to setup on your website.

Once a customer buys the drop shipping product from your website you'll then go to the drop shipping service buy the product the customer bought from your website, send the drop shipper service the delivery details and they'll send the product to your customer and you'll pocket the difference.

I have a list of drop shipping services I have at http://dominicbfrost.com/drop-shipping-services/.

Using drop shipping services may sound like a great service to use in order to make some money but you'll need to do your research before signing up to them as there are a lot of problems that might occur.

What Problems Might I Face When Using Drop Shipping Services?

Firstly there are a lot of scam drop shipping services out there which will sell you product at retail price rather than commercial price and they may even ask for a one off or monthly payments which you should never accept as most drop shipping services are free.

You'll need to ensure the products they send are of good quality as they may send either second hand or broken versions of the products and you have to make sure they deliver the products to the customer as there are some scam drop shipping services that will just take your money and run.

You'll have to deal with customer complaints, returns and some products may be out of stock so you'll have to contact the customer and tell them the product isn't available at the moment and they can either cancel the order or wait until it becomes available which may get you bad reviews.

Finally the product will likely be cheaper somewhere else as the drop shipper service is probably offering a wholesale services at a cheaper price per product or another seller is selling the product at a lower price as no one is interested in buying the products from them and is trying to recoup some of their losses.

What Should You Do If You Intend To Use a Drop Shipping Service?

If you intend to use a drop shipping service then you should firstly look for drop shipping service with products which are compatible with your Kindle eBooks so if you've created Kindle eBooks about art then you should look for products that are selling art supplies.

You should then do your research on the drop shipping service so that you are 100% certain that they can provide a good service to you and your customers.

Once you are 100% satisfied with the products they sell and the service they provide you should sign up to the drop shipping service and list some of the products onto your website and within other marketplaces such as eBay, Amazon and so on

But always be aware of the other costs that are involved in selling if you choose to sell at other marketplaces.

Do You Recommend I Use a Drop Shipping Service?

If you have found a reputable drop shipping service that will drop ship products for you, the products they sell are compatible with your Kindle eBooks, you have done your research and are willing to put the work in dealing with profit margins, making orders, contacting customers, dealing with customer complaints and so on then go ahead.

However if you do not want to be burdened by doing all of this work and would rather find an easier way of selling other people's products then have a look at the affiliate marketing method which in my opinion is a much better and profitable way to make money from other people's products.

BUY AND SELL WHOLESALE PRODUCTS ON YOUR WEBSITE

This is very similar to the drop shipping method however the big difference between drop shipping and wholesale is that you will be buying the products in bulk before the customer buys the products.

You'll also be storing the products and packaging and posting the products yourself rather than having a drop shipping service do it all for you.

Are There Any Advantages To Buying And Selling Wholesale Products?

The only advantage of buying wholesale products is the cost of selling each product will be cheaper than the drop shipping service.

However you are taking a big risk with buying and selling wholesale products because if you pay for the wholesale products in bulk and you cannot sell them then you'll lose a lot of your money and you'll be left with stock you'll have to chuck away.

Would you recommend I buy and sell wholesale products on my website?

I wouldn't recommend you buy and sell wholesale products on your website unless you already selling wholesale products on your website or you've drop shipped products before and are 100% sure the products will sell well on your website.

However even if your 100% sure the wholesale products will sell well on your website you will still be taking a risk as the demand for the wholesale products may change or a big seller may decide to sell the products at a hugely reduced price and you suddenly left with no sales at all.

So buying and selling wholesale products is a very risky method of making money from your website and if I were starting out I would avoid this method as much as possible.

However if you are keen on buying products from a wholesale company then I have a list of some of them available from my website at http://dominicbfrost.com/wholesale-companies/.

PROMOTE AFFILIATE PRODUCTS AND SERVICES ON YOUR WEBSITE

This is the best method you can use to make money from your website as it requires you to sell none of your own products or services, does not require you to handle any orders or refunds or take huge risks with your own money in order to sell the products and with affiliate marketing you can make a lot of money each month.

1. Find an affiliate product or service similar to your Kindle eBooks.
2. Sign up to an affiliate program and enter your details.
3. Promote the affiliate product or service on your website by either writing a product review, an article, a banner and so on.
4. Copy and paste your affiliate link provided by the affiliate program
5. Add your affiliate links within your website where you're promoting the affiliate product or service for people to click onto (VERY IMPORTANT).

Why is it Important to Add Your Affiliate Links within Your Website?

It's important to add your affiliate links within your website because when your website visitors clicks and opens your affiliate links they will be redirected to the affiliate products or services website where they will have the opportunity to buy the product or service you are promoting

If they decide to buy the affiliate product or service you are promoting then you will receive a commission from the sale.

The website visitor will have also have downloaded a tracking cookie (which is a very small text file) onto their web browser when they clicked and opened your affiliate links.

This will allow you to receive a commission from the sale of the affiliate product or service if the visitor decides to buy the product or service at a later date unless.

1. The visitor clicks on a different affiliate link provided by someone else.
2. The cookie length expires (this can be from one day to one hundred and twenty days and in some cases even longer).
3. The cookies are deleted (some browsers and programs delete cookies automatically once downloaded).

The amount of commission you can make from the sale of the affiliate product or service is depended on the affiliate program you're using but it can range from 1% up to 100% of the sale price of the affiliate product or service.

Some affiliate products and services may also offer you bonuses if you make a lot of sales so it's a highly profitable method you can use to make money from your website.

Marketplaces such as Amazon and eBay also offer an affiliate program on most of the products they sell on their website.

You can even get a commission from the sale of your own Kindle eBooks with Amazon Associates.

Where Else Can I Post My Affiliate Links?

The affiliate agreement usually specifies where you can post your affiliate links.

However most affiliate programs prefer you to keep your affiliate links within your website because they do not want your affiliate links all over the internet.

However some affiliate programs will allow you to post your affiliate link within your social networking sites such as Twitter, Facebook, YouTube and so on.

Some affiliate programs even allow you to post your affiliate link in emails, forums and other websites.

However before you do this you should read the affiliate agreement carefully and be sure where you can post your affiliate links and check regularly for any changes to the affiliate agreement which may change regularly.

If you do post your affiliate link where you are not supposed to on the internet then the affiliate program can track where the affiliate link originated from and if they find out it's from somewhere you're not allowed to post it to then they can terminate your affiliate account and any unpaid commission will not be paid to you.

So it's best to either post your affiliate links only on your website or check the affiliate agreement so that you are 100% sure where you're allowed to post your affiliate links.

Where Shouldn't I Post My Affiliate Links?

The only place where you shouldn't post your affiliate links is within your Kindle eBooks.

Amazon does not like affiliate links within your Kindle eBooks and it can result in your Kindle eBooks being removed from Amazon.

Also if you use Amazon Associate affiliate links within your Kindle eBooks they could suspend or ban your Amazon Associates account and not pay you any commission you would have received from the last sixty days.

It's much better in my opinion to have your own website links within your Kindle eBooks where you can promote your affiliate products and services rather than adding affiliate links directly onto your Kindle eBooks.

So do not post your affiliate links within your Kindle eBooks.

What Are the Best Affiliate Program to Use?

There are many affiliate programs that offer affiliate products and services but the best types of affiliate programs are from marketplaces and here are my top three.

Amazon Associates

Amazon Associates is the number one affiliate program everyone should join.

The reason why Amazon Associates is so important to join is because you can earn a commission on top of the sale of your own Kindle eBooks if you connect the affiliate link with your Kindle eBook web pages.

You'll also receive a commission if the same visitors who clicked on your Kindle eBook affiliate links decide to buy anything else from Amazon so you could get commission for a new a computer or phone and so on.

You can also promote other related Amazon Associate affiliate products onto your website

For example if you've created some Kindle eBooks about how to become a film maker or photographer then you could promote cameras, camcorders, and so on from the Amazon marketplace onto your website and because your readers will want to visit your website to see the other Kindle eBooks you've created they may also see these other products your recommending.

What's The Commission, Bonuses, Cookie Length for Amazon Associates?

The commission you can make from the sale of Amazon products depends on the products you're selling but it's usually around f4% of the product sale price which can increase with the more sales you make.

They also have a bonus bounty commission for certain subscription such as Kindle unlimited, Amazon Prime and so on.

Finally the cookie length lasts for twenty four hours so if they click the link and buy a product two days later you won't receive any commission.

Payment can be by direct deposit or if you're applying for the Amazon Associate program abroad then they can pay you either with Amazon gift cards or by cheque.

There Is More Than One Amazon Associate Affiliate Program

Amazon is a global seller of products but like many global sellers it doesn't have just one website but many websites.

All of the Amazon website will have the same Amazon title but the extension will be based on what country you reside in so you'll have Amazon.com for the U.S. version and Amazon.co.uk for the U.K. version.

Here is a list of Amazon Associate websites available based on each country.

U.S.	https://affiliate-program.amazon.com
U.K.	https://affiliate-program.amazon.co.uk/
Canada	https://associates.amazon.ca/
France	https://partenaires.amazon.fr/
Germany	https://partnernet.amazon.de/
Italy	https://programma-affiliazione.amazon.it/
Spain	https://afiliados.amazon.es/
Japan	https://affiliate.amazon.co.jp/
Brazil	https://associados.amazon.com.br/
Mexico	https://afiliados.amazon.com.mx/
India	https://affiliate-program.amazon.in/

| China | https://associates.amazon.cn/ |

You'll notice that there are only twelve Amazon Associate countries listed and other country are not listed.

This is because although Amazon is a global seller not all countries participate in the Amazon Associates program.

Should I Join All of the Amazon Associate Programs Or Should I Only Join One?

If you can only join one Amazon Associate Affiliate Program then join the U.S. version as this is the most popular program in my experience and it's where the majority of visitors and buyers come from.

However you should join the U.K. Canada, France, Germany, Italy, Spain and Japans Amazon Associate program.

The reason why you should join all these Amazon Associate programs is because your Kindle eBooks will be selling worldwide so people will be visiting your website from all over the world and if you only have affiliate links to the U.S. Amazon Associate sites then you are limiting the amount of money you can make from Amazon Associates affiliate program.

I've left out applying for the Amazon Associate programs within China, Mexico, Brazil and India as you may run into problem when signing up to these Amazon Associate affiliate programs if you are not a resident within these countries and/or do not have a bank account residing within these countries.

However you can still try and apply to the Amazon Associate programs available within these countries and if your application gets rejected then accept the rejection and move on.

I Have Multiple Affiliate Links from Different

Amazon Associate Programs Should I Add Them All On To My Website?

If you're using multiple Amazon Associate programs you'll have multiple affiliate links to the same product and this can be an issue.

So I would recommend you either use the Amazons OneLink service or a geo-targeting link service.

What Is the Amazon OneLink Service?

Amazon Associates has built a OneLink service available at https://affiliate-program.amazon.com/onelink which will connect your U.S. Amazon Associate account to your U.K, Canada, Germany, France, Italy, Spain, Japan Amazon Associate accounts so that you can monetize the traffic from these locations.

All you have to do once you've signed up to and connected the OneLink service to your international Amazon Associate account is add the onetag JavaScript code within the footer of your website.

The OneLink service will then look through all of the U.S. Amazon Associate links within your website and will redirect your visitors who click and open the Amazon Associate links to the Amazon websites to where your visitor are located and you will still receive a commission from any products your website visitors buy from Amazon within the next twenty four hours.

So if someone from the U.K. clicks onto one of your U.S. Amazon Associate Kindle eBook affiliate links within your website they will be redirected to your U.K. Amazon Kindle eBook web page and if they decide to buy one of your Kindle eBooks you'll still get a commission from the sale.

OneLink also offers the option of finding a product which closely matches the product your marketing if it can't find the same product from where your visitors are located which is very helpful and will increase the amount of commission you make.

However so far OneLink will not connect Amazon Associate accounts in China, Mexico, Brazil and India so if you have Amazon Associate accounts within these countries you will need to use a geo-targeting link service.

More information on OneLink can be found at https://affiliate-program.amazon.com/onelink.

What Is The Geo-Targeting Link Service?

A geo-targeting link service is similar to the OneLink service however you do not need to add a JavaScript tag onto your website all you will be given is one link to post.

To use the geo-targeting link service you'll need to sign up to one of the services listed on my website at http://dominicbfrost.com/geo-targeting-link-services/

You'll then need to give the geo-targeting link service your affiliate links you have from Amazon based on each country and it will provide you with one link to add onto your website which will redirect the visitors to the Amazon websites based on where they're located and you will again receive a commission for any sale they make within twenty four hours.

One of the advantages of this is that you do not have to add any code to the footer of the website and you'll only be given a one link to add onto your website.

You can also use the geo-targeting link service with Amazon Associate sites from China, Mexico, Brazil and India which you can't do with OneLink.

Be Careful When Using the Geo-Targeting Link Service

There is one big problem with using geo-targeting link service which is due to the operational agreement with Amazon Associates.

It basically says you cannot use URL shorteners if you do not make it clear that the visitor will be redirected to Amazon and technically a geo-targeting link is also a URL shortener service.

The best way to avoid this is to mention in the content that "this product is available on Amazon at (geo-targeting link)".

This complies with their agreement as you are mentioning that they will be redirected to Amazon when they click the link.

However the operational agreement regularly changes and your geo-targeting links may once again not be allowed within the program.

What Should I Use the Amazon OneLink Service or the Geo-Targeting Link Service?

If you have not signed up to Amazon Associate accounts within China, Mexico, Brazil or India or you already have a lot of U.S. Amazon Associate affiliate links within your website then you should use the OneLink service.

However if you do have Amazon Associate accounts within China, Mexico, Brazil or India then you should look at using a geo-targeting link service.

You should also use the geo-targeting link service when posting your affiliate link at other places on the internet however you should be very careful when doing this.

Where Can I Post My Amazon Associate Links?

The best place to post your affiliate links would be within your own website and nowhere else as Amazon doesn't want you to spam your link everywhere especially within email, forums and other forms of advertising.

However Amazon is opening up to the use of using affiliate links within social media accounts you control.

So you can technically post your Amazon affiliate link onto Twitter, Facebook, YouTube and so on.

However there is a problem with this which is that most social media websites don't like affiliate links posted all over there account and you may need to provide proof to Amazon that you are in control of the social media accounts.

For instance twitter has a lot of accounts in different names so Amazon will only accept Twitter accounts which have been verified.

YouTube is another service you can use as long as it's a review video and not primarily for advertising purposes which can result in your video being removed and if you repeatedly break their rules your account will either be suspended or terminated.

It's much better in my opinion to use social media, email and forums and so on to post information and links directly to your website and to keep all of your affiliate links within your website for your website visitors to click onto.

What Else Should I Know About Amazon Associates Affiliate Program?

Amazon had a problem of people promoting free Kindle eBooks with affiliate links.

So if Amazon Associates finds out that your website is primarily promoting free Kindle eBooks and there are a lot of people who have downloaded free Kindle eBooks from your affiliate links then it may not pay out the commission for that particular month.

The best way to avoid this is to regularly check Amazon Associates to see how many free Kindle eBooks are downloaded from your Amazon Associates program and if it starts to reach over a few thousand then you'll need to look at removing the affiliate links associated with your free Kindle eBooks and if it still becomes an issue then remove the affiliate links associated with all your Kindle eBooks.

This is nothing to worry about when starting out but even if you get a lot of free downloads then you're probably getting a lot of Kindle eBook sales and will not need to attach affiliate links to the books.

The Amazon Associate Program, OneLink and Geo-Targeting Link Service Is Too Complicated

If you find this all too complicated then Amazon OneLink services have tutorials available at the following links https://affiliate-program.amazon.com/help/node/topic/202164400?cid=integrationguideonelinkintllp&ac-ms-src=integrationguideonelinkintllp

More information on how to use the geo-targeting link service can also be found at https://affiliate-program.amazon.co.uk/promotion/geotargeting.

Finally Amazon has tutorials on how to join there Amazon Associate Program at https://affiliate-program.amazon.com/welcome/topic/tools/ref=amb_link_472781542_2 and it has a discussion forum at https://engagedforums.com/discussions/Amazoncom_Associates/am-associhelp?redirCnt=1&=.

EBay Partnership Program

The eBay Partnership program which is available at https://partnernetwork.ebay.com/ is very similar to Amazon Associate program as it has a wide range of physical products which you can promote, the cookie lasts for twenty four hours and if someone buys an alternative product from eBay within that time you will still make a commission from the sale.

There are however some small differences which are firstly the amount you can make from a sale is around 40% to 70% of eBay's revenue and you'll only need to create one account to be eligible to use eBay partnership program worldwide.

You can also market affiliate products on your social media accounts as long as you tell eBay what accounts you have and how you intend to market them on YouTube, Google+ Pages, Twitter, Facebook Pages and so on.

But do not post affiliate links within Facebook Groups, Google+ Communities and any other social accounts you are not in control with.

Although all of this may sound better than Amazon Associates there are still some problems.

What Sort Of Problems Can I Encounter When Using the EBay Partnership Program?

The first problem you will encounter is the traffic to your website will mostly come from people who have bought or downloaded your Kindle eBooks so you know that the traffic you drive to your website will be more willing to buy from Amazon rather than eBay.

However although the majority of your website traffic will be from your Amazon it does not mean no one visiting your website will buy from eBay.

The best thing to do in my opinion is if you see the same product available at both Amazon and eBay then market the product at both stores.

So you can write on your website "this product is available from Amazon at (Amazon affiliate link) and on eBay at (eBay affiliate link)" this will give the visitors the option to decide which marketplace they prefer to buy from.

You can also write something simple like "this product is available at the following marketplaces

Amazon (Amazon affiliate link)
EBay (eBay affiliate link)"

The second problem you will encounter is to do with the affiliate link you use as eBay doesn't allow you to use short linking services except for Google. Twitter, Facebook and Bitly.

So you cannot use the geo location link service.

The reason why it's a problem is because although the affiliate program is available worldwide you still have to specify the location you want to market such as U.S., U.K. Canada and so on.

So if you decide to market a product from the U.S. and a U.K. visitor from your website clicks and opens your affiliate link and decides to leave the U.S. version of eBay and visit the U.K. version of eBay and buys the product then you will not get any commission.

Also even if the seller from the U.S. does sell the product they may not ship internationally and even if they did the cost of shipping is more expensive so the visitor is more than likely to either not buy the product or visit the eBay website where they're located and buy the product from their instead

However there are solutions as eBay is now offering a geo location search term link service.

What Is the Geo Location Search Term Link Service?

Basically more than one seller will likely be listing for the same product you want to promote on your website so on the eBay partnership program you'll need to select the link generator section and select the search term radio button.

You'll then need to type the product keywords and then select the geo location radio button.

When you have done this and filled in the other details and selected the generate link you will be given an affiliate link.

When a visitor clicks on the affiliate link they will be redirected to eBay where they are located and they will see a list of the products based on the search term you entered from multiple sellers and if the visitor buys any of the products within twenty four hours you will receive a commission from the sale.

However the geo location service is only available to U.S., U.K., Canada and Australia but it's better than having multiple links.

Also when entering the search term you'll need to make sure that it shows the product you want to promote because if another product appears this can have an effect on the affiliate money you can make from your affiliate link.

Should I Use the EBay Partnership Program?

It's up to you whether or not you want to use the eBay partnership program but it is a very good alternative to Amazon Associates affiliate program and it's one I recommend you use in conjunction with Amazon Associates.

Clickbank

Clickbank is a worldwide affiliate marketing platform designed specifically to promote digital products. The products range from eBooks, audio, video and software and so on.

They're also starting to sell physical products such as books, DVD's, CD's, health supplements and so on.

Clickbank is very different from Amazon and eBay because the products are not hosted within Clickbank website they're hosted on the product creators' website.

Also you will not get commission for the other products within Clickbank apart from the product you are promoting.

So if you were promoting a product about keeping fit and a visitor clicks and opens your affiliate link and doesn't buy the product but later visits a dating guide that's part of Clickbank affiliate program and buys the dating guide then you will not receive a commission

The only way you will receive a commission is if the website visitor decides to go back to the original keeping fit product you were promoting and buys it.

However there are a lot of benefits when promoting Clickbank affiliate products.

What Are The Benefits To Using The Clickbank Affiliate Program?

Firstly the amount you can make depends on the vendor but it can be as high as 75% of the sale and the product costs can range from a few dollars to hundreds of dollars.

The tracking cookie that Clickbank adds to the visitors' browser lasts for sixty days which is a lot longer than Amazon or eBay so if a visitor returns to the website and doesn't delete the cookie or clicks onto another affiliate link and decides to buy the product your promoting within the sixty day period you will receive a commission from the sale.

You can find vendors who will also offer upsell products to their customer which basically means that after the sale of their product the vendor will try and get the buyer to purchase another product they've created which you'll also receive a commission for which means a lot more money to you.

You can also find recurring paying product which means the customer will be charged daily, weekly, monthly or yearly and you'll receive a commission every time the customer is charged.

You do not have to use any geo targeting link service as you will get a commission regardless as to where the visitor is from.

The vendor may also provide you with a lot of material in order to promote their affiliate product for instance they may give you email templates, banners, videos, mp3, eBooks, articles, press release, landing pages and a lot more.

Finally you can promote most of the affiliate products on Clickbank on forums email, social networks and so on.

How Do I Find Products on Clickbank to Promote?

You will need to do the following.

1. Create an affiliate account with Clickbank by visiting https://accounts.clickbank.com/signup/.
2. Enter your details.
3. Visit Clickbank affiliate marketplace at https://accounts.clickbank.com/marketplace.htm and type keywords related to your Kindle eBooks find product search engine and then click the search button.

When you have done this you will see a list of affiliate products which you can promote but before you do this you should click and open the links in order to visit the vendors' product website and see whether it's an affiliate product you want to promote.

When you have found the affiliate products you want to promote then you'll need to do the following.

1. Go back to Clickbank search page and click and open the promote button next to the affiliate product you intend to promote.

2. Another Clickbank web page will then open up asking you for your account nickname which you'll need to enter.
3. Press the create button.

You'll be have your affiliate link which you will need to copy and paste onto your website and use to promote the affiliate product.

Choosing a Product on Clickbank to Promote

You have to do your research when signing up to and promoting certain products within Clickbank as although Clickbank has a lot of great products to sell within their program there are still a few which are not worth promoting because of the amount of complaints, refunds they receive.

This can have a bad effect on your website and your reputation.

The best way to ensure the product is of good quality is to contact the owner of the affiliate product and ask for a free review copy of their products.

However some product owners may be unwilling to offer you a free review copy of their products especially if you're just starting out.

You could buy the product yourself but the cost of some of the products on Clickbank can be high and it's not worth wasting money just to determine whether a product is worth promoting.

So the best method you can use if you can't get hold of a review copy of their product is to firstly check the website and see what they're selling, whether the product looks good, whether the website looks professional and stands out.

You should then check the vendor stats and see how long they have been operating for and the gravity number.

The higher the gravity number then the more sales it's getting which means the product is popular.

Finally check how much you'll be earning from the sale of the products. I recommend you look for products that offer you at least 50% of the sale price with either upsells so they will be making more than the initial sale or a product with recurring payments so you'll earn more from the same customer as long as they remain a loyal customer.

Once you've done all of this you'll then need to come to a decision as to whether you want to promote the product or not.

This is something you'll need to think about because if a product is rubbish then although at first you'll get some sales you'll start to see refunds coming in which will mean the money you thought you were earning will be going back to the customer.

Your reputation may also be diminished if you start promoting products which are all rubbish or full of scams so you will need to be careful.

Do You Recommend I Promote Products from Clickbank?

Although there are a lot of problems to promoting Clickbank affiliate products such as not getting commission for the full range of products Clickbank has and the fact that you have to research the quality of the product your promoting due to refunds complaints and so on there are a lot of upsides such as the price of products, commission percentage and cookie length.

So I would recommend you promote products on Clickbank if you find a product related to your Kindle eBooks and is of good quality with minimal refunds, complaints and so on.

Other Affiliate Products and Marketplaces

I have a list of affiliate products and marketplaces on my website at http://dominicbfrost.com/affiliate-programs-products-and-services-

available/ or you can easily just visit Google type a keywords related to your Kindle eBooks with the words "affiliate program" at the end and you will have a list of products that offer affiliate programs.

What Affiliate Product and Marketplaces Do You Recommend I Promote?

The only affiliate marketplace I recommend every Kindle eBook author/publisher should use is Amazon Associates.

The reason why I recommend the Amazon Associates affiliate program so strongly is because the Kindle eBook links within your website can also be part of the Amazon Associates affiliate program.

So if a visitor on your website clicks onto one of your Kindle eBook links and buys one of your Kindle eBooks you will not only make money from the sale of your Kindle eBooks but you'll also receive a commission from the sale of your own Kindle eBook as well.

You'll also receive commission for any other product that visitor buys within twenty four hours which will mean you could receive more which is why Amazon Associates is the number one affiliate program everyone who's created a Kindle eBook should join.

As for the other products and marketplaces you use to promote affiliate product it really depends on what sort of Kindle eBooks you've published.

For instance if your fictional Kindle eBooks are within the science fiction genre and about aliens then you could look at promoting alien type merchandize from Amazon or eBay or other affiliate products available on the internet.

If however you've created some non-fictional books then you should look at marketing affiliate products that compliment your Kindle eBooks

So if you've created some Kindle eBooks about how to play golf then you should be promoting golf clubs, golf balls, golf bags, golf buggies and even golf membership clubs from Amazon, eBay and other places on the internet.

You could also look at products very similar to your own Kindle eBooks but in a different format for example you could find someone who has created a series of golf video tutorial on Clickbank or other marketplaces and promote their product on your website.

However try and avoid promoting Kindle eBooks from other authors especially Kindle eBooks which are in direct competition with yours as your readers and website visitor may decide it's better to read their Kindle eBooks rather than yours and you may end up with less regular Kindle eBook readers.

INSERT ADVERTS WITHIN YOUR WEBSITE

Inserting adverts whether its text or image based within your website is another way you can make money.

You can make money from the adverts either when a visitor click on the adverts or with every thousand web page impression the advert is placed within your website.

You can also make money from adverts on daily, weekly, monthly basis.

Inserting adverts onto your website is a long term strategy which shouldn't be over used as website visitors do not like too many adverts being added onto a website and your main goal is to sell your Kindle eBooks or other products and services you either selling or promoting on your website.

It's also not a good route if you're just starting out as you won't have much traffic to your website until you have marketed your website for a while and have a range of published Kindle eBooks.

If you are just starting out then I recommend you put Amazon Associate links and Amazon CPM ads onto your website.

What Are Amazon CPM Ads?

Amazon is not only paying you when a visitor clicks on an affiliate link from your website and buys a product. It's also now paying you for every thousand web page advert impression within your website.

All you have to do is sign up to the program at https://affiliate-program.amazon.com/home/cpmads/introduction?ac-ms-src=ac-nav then create the ad codes and copy and paste the code into your website. More information can be found at https://affiliate-program.amazon.com/help/node/topic/202116930.

The pay is dependent on the website you've created and the amount of traffic you have coming into your website so you're unlikely to make a lot of money if you're just starting out.

However Amazon CPM ads are still a good method to use when the traffic to your website increases and it can be a good way to gain a passive income from your website.

Are There Any Other CPM Advertisers?

I have a list of other advertisers on my website at http://dominicbfrost.com/advertising-programs/ which also contains a list of cost per click advertisers and other advertising schemes.

What Is Cost Per Click Advertising?

Cost per click works in the same way as CPM however the big difference is you will not make money per thousand impressions but per click so your website visitor have to click on the advert for you to make any money from the advert.

The most popular cost per click program is Google AdSense and it's one which I recommend you use if you intend to use a cost per click advertising program.

However if you're not comfortable using Google AdSense then there are others available from my website at http://dominicbfrost.com/advertising-programs/.

What Are the Other Advertising Methods Available?

You could sell advertising space directly from your website either daily weekly or monthly.

In order for you to do this you would enter the following text in the area where the advert could be added "this advertising space is available to buy click here for more details".

When someone clicks the link they will be redirected to your advertising page where you show your statistical information such as the amount of visitors, age, gender and so on.

You'll also need to add the other places where their ad can appear, the content restrictions and your rate card which will be the costs you will charge for the adverts to appear on your website.

You can either ask them to contact you or you can charge them directly from your website when an advertising space is available.

The more traffic you receive from your website the more you can charge.

There are even sites that you can use to advertise your free ad space such as Buysellads.com.

However I recommend you sell advertising space directly onto your website if you are going down the route.

Affiliate marketing is also technically an advertising method you can use but I've already been through this in the previous chapter.

What Advertising Program Do You Recommend I Use?

I recommend again if you are just starting out that you use either use Amazon Associates affiliate program and then later on start using Amazon CPM ads.

However when you start getting a lot of traffic to your website you should look at exploring other avenues and try to test them out.

For instance you could insert Google AdSense advertising onto your website for a week and if the revenue isn't as high as the other methods you're using then you should remove the advert from your website and try another advertising method.

You should also see whether people are interested in buying your advertising space within your website by adding in the contact section an advertising email address and if there are a lot of email message requests then you should consider using this method in order to make some more money.

However again do not put too much advertising on your website as visitors do not like websites with too many advertising and your main goal is to sell your Kindle eBooks along with other products and services.

WHICH METHODS SHOULD YOU USE TO MAKE MONEY FROM YOUR KINDLE EBOOKS AND WEBSITE

The methods everyone should use to make money from their Kindle eBooks are as follows.

- Create and sell a Paperback version of your Kindle eBooks.
- Amazon KDP Select enrolment.
- Promote your Kindle eBooks on your website.
- Provide a free email newsletter service.
- Use the Amazon Associates affiliate program.

You have to use these methods as they are the best methods you can use to make money from your Kindle eBooks.

The only variable comes from the other methods and it really depends on your circumstances and the type of Kindle eBooks you've created.

For instance if you've published fictional books then you should also look at doing the following.

- Create an audio version of your Kindle eBooks.
- Use services such as Cafepress and Spreadshirt to create a product range and add your book covers onto the merchandize.
- Add Amazon CPM ads and other adverts when your website traffic increases.
- Try and sell the film and television rights to your Kindle eBooks once it's gained a lot of sales and five star reviews.

If however you've published non fictional books then you could look at doing the following.

- Promote affiliate products similar to your Kindle eBook.
- Insert adverts such as Amazon CPM ads, cost per click or privately selling ad space onto your website when your website traffic increases.
- Create and sell a digital product or membership service when you the time and a vast range of published Kindle eBooks on Amazon.

If however you are a web designer and have published a Kindle eBooks about creating websites then you should look at doing the following.

- Sell website templates you've created.
- Sell your services as a web designer.
- Look at promoting a web hosting program through the use of an affiliate program.

So you need to examine the Kindle eBooks your publishing and your circumstances and decide what methods are best for you.

CONCLUSION

Now that you know the different methods you can use to make money from your Kindle eBooks you may be thinking that it's time to put all of this in place and start making some money right now.

However before you do this you will need to study your Kindle eBooks and decide which methods you should use to make money from your Kindle eBooks?

You should also look at the short, medium and long term you can use in order to make money from your Kindle eBooks and work towards implementing them.

And finally it is essential that you market your Kindle eBooks and your website in order for you to start making money from your Kindle eBooks.

If you do not bother marketing your Kindle eBooks or website then no one will be buying your Kindle eBooks or the products and services you are selling and marketing from your website as no one will even know your Kindle eBooks and website even exists.

Which is why I recommend you buy my [Kindle Marketing Victory](#) book which will show you some of the best methods you can use to market your Kindle eBooks and website.

THANK YOU

Finally I'd like to say thank you for buying my book.

If you enjoyed reading book then I'd really appreciate it if you would post a short review on Amazon by visiting the link below.

https://www.amazon.com/dp/B07B7NKS67

Also please check out my other Kindle and Paperback books available in the following pages and check out my websites at http://dominicbfrost.com/ for more information and updates.

Dominic. B. Frost

http://dominicbfrost.com/

Facebook: https://www.facebook.com/Dominic-B-Frost-1486663614766022/

Twitter: https://twitter.com/DominicBFrost

OTHER BOOKS

Available To Buy From Amazon At
https://www.amazon.com/dp/B07B7NKS67
Get Your Copy Now

Available To Buy From Amazon At
https://www.amazon.com/dp/B07B7PPYS2
Get Your Copy Now

Available To Buy From Amazon At
https://www.amazon.com/dp/B07B7NX43W
Get Your Copy Now

www.ingramcontent.com/pod-product-compliance
Lightning Source LLC
Chambersburg PA
CBHW070200230526
45471CB00002B/749